Scotland

Edited By Sarah Washer

First published in Great Britain in 2018 by:

 Young**Writers**

Young Writers
Remus House
Coltsfoot Drive
Peterborough
PE2 9BF
Telephone: 01733 890066
Website: www.youngwriters.co.uk

FOREWORD

Welcome Reader, to *Rhymecraft - Scotland*.

Among these pages you will find a whole host of poetic gems, built from the ground up by some wonderful young minds. Included are a variety of poetic styles, from amazing acrostics to creative cinquains, from dazzling diamantes to fascinating free verse.

Here at Young Writers our objective has always been to help children discover the joys of poetry and creative writing. Few things are more encouraging for the aspiring writer than seeing their own work in print. We are proud that our anthologies are able to give young authors this unique sense of confidence and pride in their abilities as well as let their poetry reach new audiences.

The editing process was a tough but rewarding one that allowed us to gain insight into the blooming creativity of today's primary school pupils. I hope you find as much enjoyment and inspiration in the following poetry as I have, so much so that you pick up a pen and get writing!

Sarah Washer

CONTENTS

Sidlaw View Primary School, Dundee

Keira Berry (9)	60
Khianna McLeod (9)	61
Evelyn Brown (9)	62
Lauren Christie (9)	63
Hannah White (8)	64
Faith Milne (9)	65
Rhiley Whyte (9)	66
Faith Davies (9)	67
Aidan Ellington (8)	68
Adam Heggie (9)	69
Marshall Quin Thomson (9)	70
Lexie McMillan (8)	71
Wyatt Scott Reynolds (9)	72
Bryony Betty Gladys Charmain Lyons (9)	73
Lucy Gillan (9)	74
Kasey Wilson (9)	75
Jenna Boyle (9)	76
Robyn Esplin (8)	77
Beau Finlayson (8)	78

St Aloysius Primary School, Chapelhall

Daniel Kinta	79
Gemma Hickey (9)	80
Jayden Tolmie (10)	82
Faith Oswald Mcindoe (9)	83

St Martha's Primary School, Glasgow

Sophie Sandra Gannon (9)	84
Nana-Ama Agyemang-Mintah (8)	85
Kai Nisbet (8)	86
Lennin Duffy (8)	87
Eve Kilshaw (9)	88
Amber Marie McColl (8)	89
Rebecca Hannah (7)	90
Zahrah Babalola (8)	91
Cianna Smith (9)	92

Maicie Louise Kennedy (9)	93
Ben Scouller (8)	94
Lewis Stirling	95
Karys Early (8)	96
Thomas John Paterson (8)	97
Kelsey Flannigan (8)	98
Cox Collins-Clarke (7)	99
Kyle George Jack Liam John Scott (8)	100
Sophie Travers (8)	101
Ajay Greenhill (8)	102
Connor Nelson (8)	103
Niamh Isabel Kelly (8)	104
Aaron Stirling (8)	105
William McGrath (8)	106
Abel Sunil (7)	107
Michael Thomas Douglas (8)	108
Ashley Bryson (8)	109
Calvin Greenhill (8)	110
Ryley John McColl (8)	111

St Monans Primary School, St Monans

Erin Clarke (9)	112
Anya Renwick	114
Amy Elder (10)	115
Jay Ketchen (10)	116
Kacey Greig (11)	117
Eva McKend (10)	118
Esha Ahmed (10)	119
Georgia Syme (9)	120
Archie Taylor (11)	121
Andrew Ireland (10)	122
Hollie Brown (9)	123
Sean Scott (11)	124

The Glasgow Academy, Milngavie

Callum Douglas Taylor (8)	125
Cora Welstead (8)	126
Callum Aitken	127
Lily Teale (8)	128
Sebby Cauchi (7)	129

Whithorn Primary School, Whithorn

THE POEMS

Colours

Life is full of colours
They are everywhere
In our surroundings
In our friends
In ourselves and in our thoughts
There are colours everywhere

Whether the colour is as dull as coal
Or as bright as the sun
Whether it's blue or green
There are colours everywhere

I like to think that it is the thought that counts
But without the colour it just isn't right
There are colours everywhere
Do you like colours?
Because I think that you do
For what is life without a touch of blue?

Rosie May Hogg (11)
Langholm Primary School, Langholm

Dreams Come True

This is a recipe for a dream, enjoy!

Firstly put a pinch of ideas
Put it in a bowl and then pour in some creativity
Along with some determination
Before whisking together

Next add in some motivation
Along with some hard work and effort
Crack in some commitment and whisk again

Then sprinkle in some enterprising skills
And some sweetness to make it more appealing
Before adding a good sized chunk of ambition
And mix once more

Line your baking tin with baking paper
And pour your mixture in before setting your oven
heat to 17° of potential
And bake for 15-20 minutes
Take it out of the oven and decorate however you
like, and bingo!
Your dream cake is done

Serve as desired
Any dream can come true with this recipe.

Olivia Boustead (10)

Langholm Primary School, Langholm

I Am A Knight

I have my sword at my side and my steel plate armour
I have my bow on my back with my arrows at its side
Fight with pride at my king's side
I worked hard to become a soldier, a trooper
Or whatever you want to call it
I have my dagger in hand, eye-to-eye with my foe
I protect the king
Sometimes people ask, 'What are you then?'
'Who me? Oh, I'm a knight!'
I have courage
I have fate
I have loyalty
I care
I fight
I sneak
I obey the king
I am a knight.

Ruby Lockwood (10)
Langholm Primary School, Langholm

Autumn

Thousands of leaves fall onto the ground
Blizzards of orange swirling round and round
Mushrooms bursting out just to be found
It's autumn
It's autumn

I see a badger snuffling around a tree
I see a squirrel staring at me
I see a fox, sly as can be
It's autumn
It's autumn

There are lovely sights waiting for you
It's great fun though, the fact that summer's
through
The shout of a girl, the cry of a ewe
It's autumn
It's autumn.

Màiri Hanley (10)
Langholm Primary School, Langholm

Animals

A nimals are adventurous, animals are strong

N arwhals are incredible, narwhals are awesome, but best of all is their spiky horn

I ndian elephants weigh a lot, up to 5,000kg!

M onkeys, they're cheeky and mischievous, watch your lunch before they eat it!

A nts, they're small but vicious, don't let them bite you

L ions are the kings of the animal kingdom

S lugs are slimy, slugs are slippy, watch out for their slippery trail!

Ben Borthwick (11)

Langholm Primary School, Langholm

Spring

In the spring
The leaves come out
And cover all the bare trees
Then rustle in the wind
As if they are all clapping

In the spring
The lambs are born
And leap around their fields
Startling all the birds away
Back to their nests up high

In the spring
The flowers bloom
And meadows come alive
Corn is also growing
And the harvest mouse is busy
As all her babies need feeding
Just as much as her.

Emily Bonser (11)
Langholm Primary School, Langholm

Friendship Cake Recipe

This recipe will teach you how to make the amazing friendship cake!

Take a spoonful of courage
Pour some strong kindness
Sprinkle some intelligence inside your mixture
Now whisk all your ingredients until smooth
Put your friendship delicious mixture in a cake tray and put in the oven for 15 minutes
When your cake is done, leave it to cool
Afterwards, pour some scrumptious icing on your cake and also add your cherry on top.

Payton Irving (11)

Langholm Primary School, Langholm

Football

F ootball, football is very fun

O wn goals are bad for your team

O Blak is a very good goalkeeper

T ackles are very easy to do

B anging a shot will probably go in

A ssists are very good

L earning football, you will probably enjoy it

L eaning back in football, the ball will go higher and if you lean forward the ball will go lower.

Lewis Hall (11)

Langholm Primary School, Langholm

Football Dreams

F ootball is very fun

O n a Thursday I play this sport

O n a football pitch there are eleven players

T ackle is what you make in football

B all is what you play with

A nyone can play this sport

L ots of people play this sport

L ionel Messi is a very famous footballer.

Calum Ritchie (10)

Langholm Primary School, Langholm

All Different Animals

There are all different animals
Bears are big
Mice are small
All animals, big and small

There are all different birds
Birds of prey
Birds of many different types living today

There are all different pets
Cats with claws
Dogs with big ears
All different pets living their way.

Bethany Harper (11)
Langholm Primary School, Langholm

The Slithering Snake

S lithering Snake went up to the hen house

N abbed himself a hen or two

A fter that he went back to the hen house

K illed all the chicks and hens and ate them all for tea

E nding the snake was near, the farmer set a trap and when the snake came, *bang! Bang!* The snake was dead.

Will Donaldson (10)

Langholm Primary School, Langholm

Weather, Weather

W eather is sometimes good or bad

E vaporation is when the sun sucks up the water from everywhere

A black cloud means rain

T he sun makes me happy

H ailstones can hurt people if they are outside

E veryone enjoys fun in the snow

R ain gets everywhere soaking.

Robert Wood (11)

Langholm Primary School, Langholm

My Point Of View

Minecraft, Minecraft
My point of view - it's terrible
Some people think it's good
But there are better games
Just trust me!

It is a world full of
Lots of cubes and blocks
You can place them, break them
Do stuff with them
That's my point of view.

Seth Brown (10)
Langholm Primary School, Langholm

The Minecraft Poem

Hey yo! I'm playing this Minecraft game
We all built a house, they're all the same
Get an eye of an Ender
Go to the Nether
Don't mine through the night
'Cause creepers are in sight
Don't get in Enderman's way
Because you'll be his prey.

Jake Jarzyna (10)

Langholm Primary School, Langholm

Wolves

In the morning the wolves are gone
But when the sun goes down
The wolves roam in their forest home
Then when the full moon comes to sight
They start to howl at night
Although you think they're frightening
They also have lots of grace.

Shannon Lake (10)

Langholm Primary School, Langholm

Balloons

B eautiful colours in the sky
A ll rising gracefully
L ook at them soar through the air
L ovely bold balloons
O ver the clouds they go
O ver the land they go
N o balloon is left behind.

Marlie Mitchell (10)

Langholm Primary School, Langholm

Animal

A nimals are fearless

N arwhals have a horn like a unicorn

I ndependent animals stay on their own

M ammals are extinct, like dinosaurs

A nimals are unique

L et's watch an animal documentary.

Callum Sterling (10)

Langholm Primary School, Langholm

Animals

A nimals are beautiful

N ice but dangerous

I f you get too close to some, you

M ight not come back

A nimals are dangerous

L ots of them will kill

S low or fast, survive or die!

Lewis MacKenzie (10)

Langholm Primary School, Langholm

The Cat And Dog Poem

A diamante poem

Dogs
Cute, warm
Fluffy, playful, joyful
Sleepy, barking, shy, adventurous
Miaowing, furry, climbing
Lazy, purring
Cats.

Tiago Santos (9)

Langholm Primary School, Langholm

Quidditch

I zoom through the air
Playing it fair
Hermione and Ron cheering
My charcoal, rounded glasses fall to the ground
Making barely any sound
The Slytherins are beating us Gryffindors
It only needs me or Malfoy to get the Snitch
And chase it around the Quidditch pitch
The wind whistling as loud as a choir
As the Snitch goes higher and higher
It comes at me, I stand up on my broom
Try to grab it
Bang! Then I land on the floor
I spit a gold lump out into my hands
It's the Snitch and it drops on the floor
The judges, teachers, wizards, witches...
All shout, 'The winner is... Gryffindor.'

Courtney Smith (11)

Lybster Primary School, Lybster

Mike The Minecraft Maniac

One day in a house in the middle of a city
There lived a boy called Mike
Mike was very naughty and he liked to give people
a big, big fright
One day Mike was playing Minecraft but suddenly
he felt a tingly sensation
He was in the game surrounded by his imagination
Suddenly, he saw a figure in the distance
It was Steve eating a biscuit
'Hi!' yelled Mike but Steve did not hear it
Then out of nowhere appeared a creeper
And Mike was never seen again...
Or was he?

Eilidh McPhee (11)
Lybster Primary School, Lybster

Admire Fire And Fireworks

Fire
Quickly burning
Blaze growing bigger
The sky is fire
The world is burning alight
Sky is alive with bright colours
Sky is red, orange, yellow and brown
The fireworks were a lantern in the sky
Filling the sky with beautiful bright colours
Alive, banging, popping, squealing and screeching
Animals running in terrible fear
Making incredibly loud noises
Going up, sparking
People admiring
Fireworks.

Rhian Jemma McGuire (10)
Lybster Primary School, Lybster

Cringe City

C reeping down the cringy road
R ough as it can be, I keep on going
I then fall flat on my face
N obody came to get me
'G uys, guys!' I shouted
E very word made me hurt, nobody came

'C ome, please, I need help!'
I can hear people coming
T he whole city came to help
'Y ou came, thank you, I think I broke a bone.'

Arun Harvey Nye (11)
Lybster Primary School, Lybster

24

Mining In A Cave

M ining in a cave

 I had diamonds

N ext thing I know I'm burning to death

E ventually I am respawning

C ave, I am coming back for you

R espawning again because I fell to my death

A minute or two I got back in the cave

F urious that I lost all my diamonds

T he monsters are surrounding me, what should I do?

Billy Kennedy (10)

Lybster Primary School, Lybster

Beasts And Arrows

M inecraft was covered in ice

 I felt cold like cold milk

N ever have I seen creepers in snow

E xcited to catch the beasts

C reeping behind the creepers

R unning after them

A naesthetic dots, firing and catching them

F inally there was silence until...

T here was an Enderman... run!

Shannon Campbell (10)

Lybster Primary School, Lybster

Enderman

M ine, mine, oh no

I can spot an Enderman

N ever look him in the eye

E very time it's eerie

C raft a diamond sword to defeat him

R un away, I require some space

A m I in enough space? Well I have to be

F ight the Enderman, swing my sword

T he Enderman survived and I died.

Robert Kirk (10)

Lybster Primary School, Lybster

Minecraft

M any mobs come out at night
 I n a house you will be safe
N ever leave the house at night
E meralds and diamonds
C reate buildings, weapons and armour
R eady for battle
A fter dark you will be safe-ish
 F ast travel is an easy way to get lost
T rading with villagers.

Luc Trainer (11)

Lybster Primary School, Lybster

Happy And Sad

H appy to feel so good
A mong all my friends
P laying excitedly in fields
P lanet Earth, the planet we live on
Y ellow is after red and orange in the rainbow

S ad that the day is done
A ll my friends at home
D own in the dumps but I'll be happy again.

Lily Siggers (10)
Lybster Primary School, Lybster

I Hate Mining!

M ining in the depths

I have almost run out of torches

N obody is around to help

E very mob has tried to kill me

C reepers have succeeded

R espawned in my house

A ll my stuff is gone

F rustration is afoot

T ypical, Herobrine is at my door...

Mackenzie Gordon (11)

Lybster Primary School, Lybster

Scared!

Oh... better run quick Luis Suárez
He's the flying hawk
If you've got a bad temper, better watch out
Then try and roast me! That's cute
You lost the game, *bang!*
Luis Suárez, control your temper
We've only got two arms and we want to keep
them both.

Matthew Robertson (10)
Lybster Primary School, Lybster

In The Night

M ining in the night
I saw a zombie
N ext I shot a bow at him
E xcellent, he was dead
C reepers spawn in the night
R aging because I am near them
A dventure in the night
F rightened in the dark
T rading with villages...

Charlie Snook (11)

Lybster Primary School, Lybster

The Dream

T hat night when I was asleep in my bed, I

H ad a dream about the deep

E ating cotton candy

D reaming was amazing

R ead a sign

E at all the candy

A man with a hat

M ad he was - I ate all his candy.

Charly Coe (10)

Lybster Primary School, Lybster

Animals

A n animal is a,

N ice friendly creature.

I n the wild people love to see them roaming.

M others are protective,

A nd fathers find food.

L ovely it is to see animals.

S pring is especially lovely for animals.

Alexander Aikenhead (9)

Lybster Primary School, Lybster

Mining In Minecraft

M ining swiftly
 I n the bright and colourful
N ether until
E verything's very
C ringy and you're
R unning weird
A lex is terrible
F ree and lonely
T ree houses that fall down!

Azard Hosein (10)
Lybster Primary School, Lybster

Impact

Bang! It hits you
You don't know what to do
Here comes another one
You think it's done
Your lips are blue
If only I could fire my poo
I attempt to run
I guess being a nerd isn't so fun.

James McDougall (11)
Lybster Primary School, Lybster

Animals

A s the sun shines
N ear the freezing cold stream
I n grassy fields
M uddy cows lie
A nimals grazing happily
L ovely birds sing
S urroundings are full of life.

Lucy Coe (10)

Lybster Primary School, Lybster

Olives

Olives, olives, I love olives
Round ones, square ones, big ones, small ones
I love olives
Olives, olives, I hate olives
I will never eat them
Never have, never will!

Findlay George Foulis Gunn (11)
Lybster Primary School, Lybster

Unicorn

I saw an orange unicorn
It was munching on a thorn
It had silver flowing hair
And it was as quick as a hare
The clouds stretched to its horn.

Erin Jane McGuire (11)
Lybster Primary School, Lybster

Goats

A haiku poem

I love lots of goats
They are very cute and cool
Black ones are cutest.

Josi Meg Young (10)

Lybster Primary School, Lybster

New Friends

N ever have I met a friend so silly, they make me happy, they're real funny

E verybody loves his jokes, everyone loves her smile

W e are friends forever and ever. My

F riends are the best friends anyone could ask for, like my friends

R ight now. My friends are in a good mood and I am too

I think me and my friends are going to make cookies for

E veryone. Cookies are so good

N ow we are having a sleepover, it's so much fun

D o you know my friends' names? My friends' names are

S teven and Leah B.

Carly McLean (9)
Park Primary School, Alloa

Scary Fun

H a ha ha, I just scared her!

A s normal, I shout, 'Boo!'

L a la la, argh, a creepy doll singing!

L ying if I said I wasn't scared

O utside at night, scary costumes, saying, 'Trick or treat!'

W hee! It's so much fun

E ww, there's bodies everywhere and blood

E at all the candy in the bowl

N eigh, neigh, goes the zombie horse.

Jessica Benning (9)
Park Primary School, Alloa

Times Tables Poem

T he twelve times table

I s so silly

M arvellous and amazing

E leven times table is terrific

S o everyone loves it

T he ten times table makes me laugh out loud

A times table is where you can multiply

B eware, the sums can be hard

L earning the times table is fun

E ight times table is my favourite

S oon you'll know your times tables.

Lachlan Morris (10)

Park Primary School, Alloa

Charlie And The Chocolate Factory

R oald Dahl is my favourite author

O ompa-Loompas

A candy store

L and with candy

D own the chocolate fountain

D on't like chewing gum

A nd all of the people come to our world

H appy readers. A

L ady, Violet, turns blue by eating chewing gum.

Keira McGillion (9)

Park Primary School, Alloa

Barcelona

B arcelona is my favourite team!

A lternative boots are smart!

R eally good players in the team!

C hannel BT Sports is where you watch the football!

E veryone in the crowd is screaming

L ast night they played Celtic

O hhhh what a goal!

N ot often they get sent off

A mazing team.

Rhianna Robertson

Park Primary School, Alloa

Football

F ootball fan

O ver the net

O nly eleven people allowed

T eam Barcelona is my favourite

B est player is Messi

A ll the fans sing

L ots of goals

L ots of fun!

Abdulmalek Muhanad Alwen (9)

Park Primary School, Alloa

Candy Shop

D ancing is fun
A m I going to go to dance?
N ew moves I learn
C allie teaches me dancing
I like to dance so much
N ever ever stop dancing
G ive me some moves to dance.

Caitlyn Louise Lyons (10)

Park Primary School, Alloa

Dancing

D ancing is fun
A mie goes too
N ew moves I learn every week
C ompetitions are fun but scary
I love to dance
N ew routines are hard
G irls only.

Demi-Leigh Ferguson (9)

Park Primary School, Alloa

Rocco

R eally big fan of Rocco
O h the stunts he can do
C ool tricks on scooters
C an do flips on motorbikes
O ver two million subscribers!

Lewis Eadie (10)
Park Primary School, Alloa

The Myth That Happened Years Ago

Many years ago the ocean was as bare as a
harvested crop
Until a witch centuries old came to the seaside
To grant her last spell
As she sat at the edge of the water she muttered
the words,
'This day is my last.'
She cast a spell over the deep blue
At that moment light started to shine
Whizzing, gushing, twirling, diving
All sorts of fish and sea creatures appeared
Fish from red to purple, green to orange
Came from the twirl of light
At that moment the ocean was no longer silent.

Megan Mercer
Sandness Primary School, Sandness

Funny Puppies

P uppies are cuter than a hog

U nderdog is not a dog

P ineapple is not a dog food

P lease don't be rude and give them no food

Y oghurt is yummy but it might hurt a dog's tummy

A nimals are cute but dogs are the best

N othing is better than a puppy

D ogs are fluffy

D inosaurs are big, they might scare a dog

O ther dogs are big and small

G et a puppy now.

Simone Wilbourne

Sandness Primary School, Sandness

Hamsters Are Not Gangsters

H amsters are as fast, lucky and aggressive as gangsters

A lso, if you don't clean their cage up they stink like rotten potatoes

M ost hamsters like roller coasters and like ghost busters

S awdust makes them clean, but sadly sometimes mean

T hey are fluffy and very lonely

E verybody loves them as hamsters, not gangsters!

R ight thing to do is to buy a hamster so you're not bored.

Ryszard Pawlak (10)
Sandness Primary School, Sandness

The Little Fish And The Shark

A little fish was swimming in the ocean
He saw a shark and said, 'I'd better get going.'
He swam as fast as he could
Then he thought that he should hide
He hid under a rock and locked the lock
The shark swished his tail
And the fish, he went pale
The shark went away
And the fish, he said, 'Yay.'
The shark was quite hungry
And the fish was quite lucky
So he continued his journey.

Finn Georgeson
Sandness Primary School, Sandness

The Sea Monster!

S plashes in the water

E ating all the fish in the sea

A t midnight he goes to sleep

M ost of the time he sleeps in

O n the weekends

N ever in his life has he seen an octopus

S o today he is going to see an octopus

T ry to race him, he will win

E ven when he is tired he is fast

R oaring when he's mad.

Alice Mercer

Sandness Primary School, Sandness

Mighty Dragon

M ighty as no one

I cy and spiky

G reat and sleepy

H uge like a volcano

T all like a big mountain

Y ellow when happy

D angerous and angry

R olls and is fast

A nger keeps him safe

G iant and smart

O n he goes in the darkness

N ow he's Mr Big!

Vanja Halilovic (10)

Sandness Primary School, Sandness

Nature's Everywhere

N ature is as lovely and lively as a steady lake

A nd it has lots of life, as much as an octopus

T he octopus has three hearts, one more than two men

U nder the sea there is nature too

R emember the sea is natural and it's blue

E verywhere there's nature, even in space.

Alisher Abuladze Andreivich (10)

Sandness Primary School, Sandness

The Little Rabbit

A small, furry rabbit
Had a big habit
Liked jumping but hated bumping
He ran fast but was always last
Lived in a colourful house but always found a
mouse
Once he met a cat, he had a big, furry hat
Sharp claws and big, furry toes
He was hungry, very hungry
And chased the rabbit away.

Estera Pawlak
Sandness Primary School, Sandness

The New Iron Man

I ron Man is as tall as a skyscraper
R oman warriors are fighting like mad
O h man, he's big
N ew York City is in danger!

M ost biggest Iron Man
A nd the only one
N ew edition!

Liam Garrick (8)
Sandness Primary School, Sandness

Planes Fly

The planes fly high in the sky,
They fly gracefully in the sky,
Thunder and lightning
And they still got there,
The engine buzzes like a bee,
As we drink our hot tea
And look at the sea.

Sophie Hankin (8)
Sandness Primary School, Sandness

Minecrafter's Life

Digging in the darkness, no shining diamonds in
sight
Keep a close watch, mobs give me a fright
Find a strange hold, it's near the end
Gain an eye of Ender from a dark, black hole in
Enderman's head
Now get some obsidian and go to the Nether
Get a blaze rod, it's not hard, it never was ever!
Now find a wither skull from a wither skeleton's
head
Now make a soul sand cross and put the skulls on
top
The wither had spawned now for a fight
It might hurt you, who cares? You might
The wither is dead, EXP is everywhere
The wither star is there in sight
Look at its glory there in the light
Now go through the end portal to fight a boss
I liked the Ender dragon with all my might
When I killed the Ender dragon it was such a
glorious sight
This, a Minecrafter's life.

Keira Berry (9)
Sidlaw View Primary School, Dundee

A Weird Day

Once there was a guy called Bobby
But he liked to be known as Bob
So Bob is what we are going to call him
That day he went to work at his job

One bright, sunny day Bob started his day
In a funny kind of way
His phone started
To ring with a ring, ring-a-ding-ding

Then he thought, *oh my phone is ringing*
Who can it be?
It started with a ring and ended with a ding
There is only one person it can be!
'Hello there Bob.'
It was his manager you see!
'What you doing?
Come quickly over here.'
The shouting from his boss gave him a flea in his
ear.

Khianna McLeod (9)
Sidlaw View Primary School, Dundee

Cool DJ's Pyjamas

C ool Colin is a cool DJ,
O nly boring DJs don't wear PJs,
O bsessed DJs are the best!
L ive like a DJ and love PJs.

D Js talk about their PJs,
J amie is DJ Stiley,
S piky hair is a DJ style.

P erfect pyjamas are preferred,
Y ounger styles are a choice.
J umping beats and slippers on his feet
A nimals' pyjamas are second choice!
M assive music notes are best,
A lways wear your PJs if you are a DJ,
S tyle yourself to be the best and beat the rest.

Evelyn Brown (9)

Sidlaw View Primary School, Dundee

Unicorns And Friends

I love fluffy unicorns
Especially the ones in uniforms
My unicorn met a cat and a bat
Who sat on a cloud all day
The cat and bat ate all clouds
Until they had all gone away
The unicorn, bat and cat fell on the ground
That made a crashing sound then they rolled onto
the mound
The mound was full of candyfloss
They ate it all until it was gone
After that they sang a song
They walked and talked until they found a special
sock
They wore that sock then fell asleep
I woke up and it was all a dream
I hope one day it can be real so I can have those
adventures in the sky.

Lauren Christie (9)
Sidlaw View Primary School, Dundee

Animals Are Magic

A nimals snap, roam, chomp and purr
N ewts can slide and swim
I ndian elephants can walk far
M y horse can walk and trot
A chimpanzee can crawl and swing
L izards can slide and crawl
S piders can make a web

A nimals purr, animals bark
N arwhal swimming in the ocean
I guana slither, iguana slide
M onkeys jump and monkeys climb
A pes can crawl, apes can jump
L ions crawl and lions roar
S nakes slither and snakes slide.

Hannah White (8)
Sidlaw View Primary School, Dundee

Friendship

Fantastic friends are funny
Friends are remarkable, right and never wrong
Friends are crazy or should I say *my* friends are!
My friends are enchanted, they do things for me
Friends are hilarious, they make you laugh all day
Friends are daft but silly in a way
Friends are smart but not all the time, I wonder if they could read this rhyme?
Friends are nice like mice creeping along to give you advice
Your friends could be popular but not all the time
All of these friends will always be mine.

Faith Milne (9)
Sidlaw View Primary School, Dundee

Friendship And Horses

In the day I play away
Looking for a way to find my hay
All day long I neigh and pray
All the month of May I pray for hay
Following May, I store it away
Saving hay for a rainy day
So I can always play my way in the hay
My best friend comes to play
In the hay for the day
We played responsibly all the month of May
We don't care, we're still smart and popular
But these are qualities not important to me, I'm
happy being me!

Rhiley Whyte (9)
Sidlaw View Primary School, Dundee

Minecraft Mines

Digging for diamond, iron, coal and normal stone
I like to mine at night and dig in the daylight
My mum told a story, that gold was glory and
diamond to her was just a story
Red stone is a miracle, it will do anything you want
I used it to open a portal to another world
In that world was a diamond house with an iron
door and a gold floor
In big, bold writing read
'Rhymecraft!'
In the sky.

Faith Davies (9)
Sidlaw View Primary School, Dundee

Untitled

At night the zombies fight
Chomper the big plant starts to bite
Chomper chomps like a monster
Daisy shoots out petals like a firework!
Cactus shoots out spikes as stabby as a shard of
wood!
Engineer fights with his paint roller and at the end
he falls off his kite
Imp Mech gets all the plants and at the end
Then he explodes
After that, he eats some toads!

Aidan Ellington (8)
Sidlaw View Primary School, Dundee

The Amazing Xbox

Once there was a little boy called Joe
He liked playing his Xbox One a lot
When he came back from the school show
The next day he invited his old friend Beau
To play alongside his go
They decided to be funny while playing the Xbox
They put on bow ties and wore funny socks
After that they put the cheesy socks
On his Xbox.

Adam Heggie (9)
Sidlaw View Primary School, Dundee

Cats And Bats

I like cats and bats
That sit on mats and take naps
And sometimes collapse
I love cats and bats that always have naps
They always collapse
I love them because they are fast and the cat is so
fluffy
I appreciate cats and bats as they nap
Because I want to copy them and collapse and
also take naps.

Marshall Quin Thomson (9)
Sidlaw View Primary School, Dundee

Sea Pony

You're very lucky if you see a ducky
But you're very, very, very lucky if you see a sea
pony
Sea ponies play all day and they play with
stingrays
Stingrays are grey
They give X-rays, they are so brave
Especially when they are in the darkness of a cave.

Lexie McMillan (8)

Sidlaw View Primary School, Dundee

Zombie Pet

At night the zombies come out and bite.
In the night the zombies come out and fight.
In the night the zombies come out to rhyme.
In the day the cat comes out to play.
In the day the dog comes out to play.
At night the cat and dog fight with all their might.

Wyatt Scott Reynolds (9)

Sidlaw View Primary School, Dundee

Rainbows And Colours

Rainbows have lots of colours
Rainbows come in green and blue
Pink colours shining through
Rainbows have lots of colours
Red, orange and yellow glowing through
Rainbows have lots of colours
Purple is the best because it is better than the rest.

Bryony Betty Gladys Charmain Lyons (9)

Sidlaw View Primary School, Dundee

Animals

A lligators have sharp teeth

N ewts are like lizards

I nsects are different sizes

M onkeys are very cheeky

A nts are very small

L ions have big manes

S eahorses are like small fish.

Lucy Gillan (9)
Sidlaw View Primary School, Dundee

Friendship

My cat sat on the mat
My dog digs up the mug
A duck said hi to the dog
The dog said hi to the duck and drank from a cup
with the cat
Can the cat give me a paw?
Can the dog run around the garden?
Can the duck quack?

Kasey Wilson (9)
Sidlaw View Primary School, Dundee

Big Bright Dreams

D ance, dance dog

R ound and round

E nergetically

A lways chasing a hound

M issing the sea full of whales

S omething is strange, something is weird, is it the sea you fear?

Jenna Boyle (9)
Sidlaw View Primary School, Dundee

Bedtime Hours

One cosy night in my bed
Two cotton pillows for my head
One comfy cover made of wool
One friendship dream is really cool
In my dream friends have magical powers
Freezing anything over my bedtime hours.

Robyn Esplin (8)

Sidlaw View Primary School, Dundee

Pandas

P erfect, prowling pandas
A mazing climbing ability
N atural habitat in China
D oesn't share his bamboo
A mazing and majestic
S haring and caring.

Beau Finlayson (8)

Sidlaw View Primary School, Dundee

The Minecraft Dream

M ysterious caves down there, coming to eat you

I n your house, terrified if creepers blow up your house

N early there but a slenderman is in your sight and you try to kill it

E ndless spiders fearing you in your spirit

C rafty diamonds looking at you very bright

R unning as fast as you can so you don't get caught by a fearless zombie

A t the shop buying all the weapons so you can kill the creatures

F inding all the cool stuff for your celebration

T hen after you go back home with the happiest day of your life and celebrate it with your friends!

Daniel Kinta

St Aloysius Primary School, Chapelhall

Endangered Animals

Animals roaming
Out in the wild
Looking for prey...
Ready to fight

From the ferocious lion
To the sneaky snake
Habitats all over the world
But people are making a mistake!

Animals, their numbers going down
From the rare Amur leopard
To the golden lion tamarin
Will these animals soon be gone?

Poachers killing animals for their fur
To make beautiful fur carpets
It depends on everyone to help
Get their population up!

The animals need you
Even the ones in the zoo!
Help the animals roam once more
It all comes down to you!

Gemma Hickey (9)

St Aloysius Primary School, Chapelhall

The Lonely Miner

I dig in the morning and until dawn
Waiting till some mobs come along.
Drinking coffee every night,
Nothing's getting out of my sight tonight!
Digging cobblestone every night
Looks like I have something to do tonight.
I see a creeper coming along
And then he blows up on my lawn.
My pumpkin patch is now gone,
Looks like I may have to buy another lawn!
I go into my house and rest up tonight,
Looks like the lonely miner has something to do
every night!

Jayden Tolmie (10)

St Aloysius Primary School, Chapelhall

Unicorn Power

Unicorn
Mythical, beautiful
Flying, flowing, hexing
Horn, wings, rainbow, fur
Glittering, sparkling
Magical, kind
Powerful.

Faith Oswald Mcindoe (9)
St Aloysius Primary School, Chapelhall

The Magical Forest

Deep down where I live, a couple of miles away
There is a little forest, quite mysterious I would say
Little gnomes and little creatures always having
fun
I wonder what happens down there, is it always as
happy and fun?
It's mostly magic but sometimes tragic
When the scary giant comes along
The animals start to shiver and they feel there's
something wrong
They start to hide, they start to tremble in fear
They don't know what's going on
But what they didn't know was the giant was nice
inside
He's been coming to the forest for years now
Just trying to find a friend
Oh how upset he was when he found out nobody
liked him
The creatures all felt bad and went to cheer him up
And they all became friends
From now on creatures and gnomes and giants all
live together in peace.

Sophie Sandra Gannon (9)
St Martha's Primary School, Glasgow

The Four Seasons

F irst, the wind's rustling and the trees are gone

O ur summer is gone until next year then we will see the sun

U se your winter coats and gloves

R euse your socks and your hats

S ee the sun glistening over you

E ars are cold, fingers are numb

A re you ever going to believe?

S ome people are at good places and they are amazed

O n the windows red, orange and yellow leaves

N ow spring has come once again

S ome animals are cold or dead, but new ones come again.

Nana-Ama Agyemang-Mintah (8)

St Martha's Primary School, Glasgow

My World

In my world I'm in charge
I build everything
Small or large
There are roller coasters and statues and a ghost train
To enter if you wish, I dare you to
For the goblins and ghosts
I built a castle
To keep them away
From my golden chapel
I dig down deep
I scaled up high
At the top of my island I created the name Kai
Come visit my island any time
But remember if you get stuck, remember your mine
I love Rhymecraft, it's a really big thing.

Kai Nisbet (8)
St Martha's Primary School, Glasgow

Minecraft

M any people in Minecraft explore caves to find diamonds and iron

I nvaders run constantly fast and sneak into your house or your mansion

N aughty people might push you down

E nderman hates water

C raft your diamonds to make tools

R eally angry feelings will make your device crash

A lso you can build a portal too

F unny and awkward people, like noobs, will build dirt houses

T rade villagers for emeralds.

Lennin Duffy (8)

St Martha's Primary School, Glasgow

Something's Missing

A nimals are ready to hibernate

N eed sleep because it is that time of the week

I s there a baby hedgehog missing? Oh no, I think it is lost

M issing animal, oh no, poor Miss Hedgehog, her name is Flo

A ll animals are special in a way, so Flo goes and looks for her baby

L eft and right she is lost but she heard a cry

S oon she found him, so on she goes with her baby, their family grows.

Eve Kilshaw (9)

St Martha's Primary School, Glasgow

Dreams

D reams are so beautiful and wonderful to think about

R is to have a remarkable dream, so wonderful, your dream is only yours

E xtreme dreams can mean you're an energetic or a sporty person

A means you're having an amazing dream about anything you think about

M arvellous things to fill your head and to dream about

S pectacular dreams, mythical things, all in your little tiny head.

Amber Marie McColl (8)

St Martha's Primary School, Glasgow

Autumn

Autumn is the best time of year
The ground is not very clear
Under the trees the leaves will fall
The trees are getting very tall
Sometimes it is sunny
People can be very funny
Everybody is going bonkers
People are looking for conkers
Conkers are falling from the trees
And so are all of the brown leaves
On Halloween we get some treats
Sometimes we dance to scary beats.

Rebecca Hannah (7)
St Martha's Primary School, Glasgow

Halloween

Halloween is the best
Can you pass your scary test?
Spiders hiding in the trees
All around the buzzing bees
Traps are hidden all around
Keep your ears peeled for a sound
Halloween is scary, I will tell you that
So scary that a snowman can melt in his top hat
Are you scared? Are you not?
You might want to give that a little thought!

Zahrah Babalola (8)
St Martha's Primary School, Glasgow

Under The Sea

In the sea there are lots of creatures
Lots of fish with different features
Some fish are big, some fish are small
But they are all God's creatures
And we love them all

Under the sea is where they live
Flowing corals all adrift
Beautiful seashells swept ashore
The sea is something I adore.

Cianna Smith (9)
St Martha's Primary School, Glasgow

The Secret Treasure In The Castle

In a land of fun and pleasure
Lives a secret castle full of treasure
Gold and silver and sparkles galore
What a wonderful place to explore
Princesses dancing in the ballroom
Hoping for a prince to become their groom
The king and the queen living the dream
Watching the servants clean, clean, clean!

Maicie Louise Kennedy (9)
St Martha's Primary School, Glasgow

Autumn

All the trees are tall
Their leaves are ready to fall
Lots of leaves to kick around
Even in my school playground
A couple of weeks, it will all clear up
With a bit of wind and the janitor
To sweep the leaves up
There are orange, red and brown leaves on the ground
So listen for a sound.

Ben Scouller (8)
St Martha's Primary School, Glasgow

My Land

C reative lands of mysteries and creatures
R un fast if you dare to escape my land
A s you walk through my land you will find buildings high and low
F ind lots of treasure and magical gems under my caves
T here are tunnels, keep digging deep if you want to find my treasures.

Lewis Stirling

St Martha's Primary School, Glasgow

Autumn

A utumn time is coming

U nder the trees, the leaves will fall

T he animals will all start to hide

U p in the trees the birds will sleep and small ants
will crawl

M ist will fill the sky quietly

N ight grows long and it gets darker so it looks
like nothing at all.

Karys Early (8)
St Martha's Primary School, Glasgow

Football

F ootball is fun

O thers playing in the sun

O ver the fence the ball will go

T he pitch is far for you to go

B oys and girls play

A mongst the players every day

L earning new tricks for all to play

L ittle sister joins in to play.

Thomas John Paterson (8)

St Martha's Primary School, Glasgow

Dance

Dance is fun
In the sun
We are small
The dance teacher is tall
Then we run
Next we turn
I am going to look
For a costume in a book
My favourite dance is hip-hop
When I try to make my body pop
Now we dance in the back hall
I do my spins and I try not to fall.

Kelsey Flannigan (8)
St Martha's Primary School, Glasgow

Games

Games are cool
Games have tools
Especially when you're in the sun
Games are always lots of fun
Games on my PS4 are best
Then I go and have a rest
Minecraft is a game I like
And then I go and use my mic
You can play with all your friends
I hope the game never ends.

Cox Collins-Clarke (7)
St Martha's Primary School, Glasgow

Minecraft

M y favourite game
 I like my character's name
N injas all around
E xciting game to play on the ground
C reepers over there
R unning over there
A wesome game to play
 F un to have all day
T ogether me and Mum play.

Kyle George Jack Liam John Scott (8)
St Martha's Primary School, Glasgow

Levis

Levis is my cat
He doesn't like the rats
Every day he grows
He doesn't like my bows
Very big chunks of food
How is it even good?
I have to feed him every day
Sometimes he tries to run away
So tiny, so cute
He has a fluffy foot.

Sophie Travers (8)
St Martha's Primary School, Glasgow

October

October is the month
When the leaves fall off the tall trees
Autumn is fun when the leaves are on the ground
You kick them and throw them
Halloween is coming and you'll have lots of fun
Scare people and have a blast!

Ajay Greenhill (8)
St Martha's Primary School, Glasgow

School

School is cool
When we follow the rules
We play on the wavy grass
Stay away from the glass
We learn all about the past
Time is going so fast
We play football in the sun
It is so much fun.

Connor Nelson (8)
St Martha's Primary School, Glasgow

Autumn

In the trees, leaves fall down
The dark, creepy forest is near the town
We need to go now, let's go this way down
I yell at the end of the aisle
'Let's go trick or treating now.'

Niamh Isabel Kelly (8)
St Martha's Primary School, Glasgow

Autumn

Autumn breeze
Blows through the trees
The leaves go from green to brown
Everyone's frown turns upside down
Animals hibernate
Underneath the gate
Oh how cold is it?

Aaron Stirling (8)
St Martha's Primary School, Glasgow

Halloween

One day it was Halloween
Then there were vampires
Many people outside were running all around
Boys and girls were really loud
Vampires running about
Mums and dads begin to shout.

William McGrath (8)
St Martha's Primary School, Glasgow

Sports

Sports are cool
But also tiring
We play football on the smooth, green, wavy grass
I can sometimes overreact
When we win a football match
We'll have a big party.

Abel Sunil (7)
St Martha's Primary School, Glasgow

Minecraft

Minecraft is fun to play
I like to have a sword with clay
Characters can fly
Above the sky
Zombies, creepers, spiders come to attack
Hide, we are under attack!

Michael Thomas Douglas (8)
St Martha's Primary School, Glasgow

Christmas

Snowmen being built and snowballs all about
Presents under the trees
Santa comes when we are sleeping
Snow is falling
Santa is leaving to make more presents.

Ashley Bryson (8)
St Martha's Primary School, Glasgow

Darts Competition

Darts is cool
In the pool
We are small
The dart board is tall
When I win
I just spin
Throw the dart on the board
That man just scored.

Calvin Greenhill (8)
St Martha's Primary School, Glasgow

Sea Creatures

In the deep, blue sea
There was a big creature
It was huge
Like a sea monster
The humans started to flee
The ocean is wide.

Ryley John McColl (8)
St Martha's Primary School, Glasgow

Powerful Emotions

My heart has sunk and I can't comprehend
What's going on in my head
My heart is as broken as shattered glass
I am as dead as a dodo that can't fly away
From its fears and worries
My life is as dull as a desert
I've messed up
I've messed up a lot
My tears never dry
But I try and I try
My private life in my dreams
They're leading off to different streams
Oh please, oh please, bring me back to the
beginning
Where I was determined and my friends were by
my side
I've given up now
All because of you
I won't forget there were other ones too
I've shared my worry now and my dreams have
come true
I learned that I love my life and so should you

If you've got a worry all you've got to do
Is tell someone that you trust
And your dreams will come true too.

Erin Clarke (9)
St Monans Primary School, St Monans

When I Look Back!

Once upon a time I was ice, I laughed in rain at others' pain
Other children kept the heat
But I had none as my soul did freeze
Maybe it was from the loneliness or the lack of cosiness
But my heart always failed to keep out the rain
Of those bitter words that I was named
They had a horrid after taste
To think I thought you were always there
But now you just don't seem to care
I thought I could laugh and cry with you
But then those tears don't seem to dry
If this is happening to you, you really must be true
Tell an adult that you trust
Because they will bring you through!

Anya Renwick
St Monans Primary School, St Monans

Life In Poverty - 18th Century London

I woke up this morning, feeling completely wrecked
My hair was all over the place and the room was an absolute pigsty
I dusted down my apron and brown dress and flattened my hair
I could smell smoke and filth coming from outside
I could hear a riot amongst the smoke and two men
I run my hand over the floor, feeling the dust and soot
The poor part of town I lived in
With contaminated air and rebellious, dangerous neighbours
Life was unfair
Me, my mother and my four little brothers and sisters
Always felt afraid and threatened.

Amy Elder (10)
St Monans Primary School, St Monans

In A Pixel World

In a pixel world, there I live
A little guy playing with no end
I battle a monster
Or go go-karting with no stop
I don't dislike this, I actually love it
So please, oh please keep on playing
I love this, I play with my friends
So keep on playing for years on end
Because your happiness is my happiness
We can go on adventures and find some items
We can build a house
We can win a race
As long as we do it together.

Jay Ketchen (10)
St Monans Primary School, St Monans

Scary World

What a scary world
A creepy alleyway
Dark houses with no light
Sad families with no food or drink
Poor families with dogs and cats on streets
Adults using different language so kids don't
understand
What a horrible feeling I get
I cry myself to sleep
I never laugh
No one makes me smile
The only thing I like is when I feel like the grass
speaks to me
What a scary world.

Kacey Greig (11)
St Monans Primary School, St Monans

Friends

You get all different types of friends
Some big and some who love to play tig
You get some old
And some who love gold
You will get some friends who would walk a mile
Just to see your smile
You will have some young
And some who hate to have fun
Some called Kacey
And some called Lacey
Also some friends can be kind
And help you find your way in life
We all need friends.

Eva McKend (10)
St Monans Primary School, St Monans

Shout And Cry

They shout and cry
I long to know why
They shout and cry while I dream
I dream of peace
Where no one shouts
And no one tells lies
Will this happen? I don't know

Then come the waterworks
I cried a flood
Mum was shocked
Dad was fearful
They stopped shouting
They stopped crying
Nothing really did matter
So we lived happily ever after!

Esha Ahmed (10)
St Monans Primary School, St Monans

Amazing Autumn

Trees become free in their imagination
Leaves chase me as I run round the street
I dive into the luxurious bed of leaves
We play tig around the big oak tree
The autumn birds make me dance as they sing all
night
All my favourite colours are the colours of the
night sky in autumn
Ask me why I love autumn?
I'm not sure why
It's just amazing.

Georgia Syme (9)
St Monans Primary School, St Monans

My Birthday!

I am writing down a poem that may get put
in a book
About my birthday
So give this page a look
There will be cake, chocolate and presents
Some twenty quid and some twenty cents
I am getting one year older
But like Granny says, 'You don't want to get old
my lad.'
But it is my birthday so...
Who cares!

Archie Taylor (11)
St Monans Primary School, St Monans

Escaping Aperture

Shooting portals, running to the exit door
Dodging the lasers of turrets!
Helping the defective turrets!
Placing down cubes
Bouncing on the repulsive gel
Being flung by the faith plates
Finding GLaDOS and destroying her
Seeing daylight for the first time, ever
This is for the people who are still alive!

Andrew Ireland (10)
St Monans Primary School, St Monans

Autumn Leaves Are Falling Down

Little leaves come falling down
Falling softly to the ground
They're swirling, twirling round the tree
As all the leaves come and dance with me
They're crashing and bashing to the ground
As all the leaves come to me
As I am jumping I can hear the leaves crunching
Crunch, crunch, crunch!

Hollie Brown (9)
St Monans Primary School, St Monans

In A Minecraft World

In a Minecraft world
Digging in a mine
In a straight line
Keep an eye out
A creeper can blow your light out
Find jewels on your right side
With your dog by your side
Get shot by an arrow
Keep the mine narrow
Start to head up
It's about to blow up
In a Minecraft world.

Sean Scott (11)
St Monans Primary School, St Monans

My Mysterious Land

M onsters rise up from the ground at night

Y ucky monsters fight strong knights

S illy citizens fighting the monsters with their special pets

T iny flowers drinking rain water

E normous forts with lots of lanterns

R hinos charge in to protect the forts

I f you see a full moon, a special temple opens

O n my land people shout, 'Charge!' for the rhinos to come

U p on top of some forts there are lookout trees

S ome forts have massive rivers around the fort

L arge trees look like guarding trees

A pples taste so good to everyone

N ever give a baby a carrot because the baby will go crazy

D ino babies like to party with the babies all night, crazy.

Callum Douglas Taylor (8)

The Glasgow Academy, Milngavie

My Lollipop Land

L ovely, colourful and tasty

O h it tastes so good, I could faint

L ollipops everywhere, I want to live here

L ove is here and it's always near

I f I could, I would eat all the lollies

P lease don't take it away today!

O ld lady and lollipop birds sitting on a lolly tree

P erfect white lolly clouds

L iving in Lollipop Land sounds amazing!

A lander bird soaring in the sky, eating a lolly

N ever take a lolly outside because

D ad will take it away in a day.

Cora Welstead (8)

The Glasgow Academy, Milngavie

My Minecraft Land

M ines underground with the scary monsters

I nside the deep, dark caverns

N ever come down here!

E at the yummy food here

C raft a massive mansion with lots of brilliant blocks

R ate it from one to ten

A t the theme park play away

F reight trains all around

T rain a pilot to fly the plane

L end a house for one day

A lligators everywhere

N oisy things all over

D o everything in this land.

Callum Aitken

The Glasgow Academy, Milngavie

My Fun Land

F abulous, fun roller coasters, fast like a cheetah!
U nderground houses, buy them while they last!
N ice smiley Mr Men as smiley as the sun

L ovely glittering rainbows everywhere you go!
A nd the waving branches on the tree
N oon time cinemas, you can get 3D
D ancing stars in the midnight sky!

Lily Teale (8)
The Glasgow Academy, Milngavie

My Lego Land

L ego men powerful and strong
E xciting as if it was born to devour
G etting fused together
O ur feelings are for you

L ego is the great big key to home you see
A nd large as can be
N early stronger than bone
D are to touch it and you will end up building
something strong.

Sebby Cauchi (7)
The Glasgow Academy, Milngavie

Monsters

Monsters run at night
They will give you a fright
Be prepared or get eaten by the monsters tonight
You better have a shiny stone sword
And trusty armour too
And if you're mining, bring a torch because
monsters roam tonight
Don't worry about the morning unless you live near
trees
Skeletons shoot you with their bows
Creepers, beware, I shall come out tonight
Endermen can take blocks so make sure you have
spare
And place torches round your house
Creepers shall blow up
Watch out for the zombies in armour
They are very strong
So be prepared for monsters to roam tonight
Zombie villagers are very smart
They shall hide
So be prepared tonight.

Aaron Lochrie (9)

Whithorn Primary School, Whithorn

The Waving Sea

The waving sea is as blue as the sky
The waves are wavy and alive
People go to the beach and play in the sand
And make a sandcastle in the shape of a clam
Go on the ship as fast as anything
One fell off and one started crying
They climbed off and got taken away by a wave
They saw their son and grabbed him tight
They climbed back onboard the ship and sailed
away back to the shore
As fast as lightning
They saw their dog and hugged with delight
Somebody shouted, 'Boo!' and gave him a fright
Then it was night
They slept in a bunk bed and they all said
goodnight.

Kacey Louise Young (7)
Whithorn Primary School, Whithorn

Mum And Dad's Renewals Day

It all started on a sunny morning
Two hearts all ready
Bonded for 25 years
Three lovely daughters
Four house moves
Many ups and downs
Hopefully bonded for the next 25 years
Have a great day
Mum and Dad
We three love you.

Shiloh Boyce
Whithorn Primary School, Whithorn

The Sun And The World

The sun is like a red power
With sparks in it like fireworks
The sun is in the sky
And puffy white clouds like marshmallows
The sea is as colourful as the sky
The trees are higher than the sea
And as colourful as the rainbow.

Stirling Ashton James Platts (8)
Whithorn Primary School, Whithorn

The Happy Pig

The happy little pig
Went to dig
To find something for tea
He found a truffle
And gave a shuffle
Then skipped home merrily.

Zack Jolly (8)
Whithorn Primary School, Whithorn

YOUNG WRITERS INFORMATION

We hope you have enjoyed reading this book – and that you will continue to in the coming years.

If you're a young writer who enjoys reading and creative writing, or the parent of an enthusiastic poet or story writer, do visit our website **www.youngwriters.co.uk**. Here you will find free competitions, workshops and games, as well as recommended reads, a poetry glossary and our blog.

If you would like to order further copies of this book, or any of our other titles, then please give us a call or visit **www.youngwriters.co.uk**.

Young Writers
Remus House
Coltsfoot Drive
Peterborough
PE2 9BF
(01733) 890066
info@youngwriters.co.uk